Leaf **Litter Critters**

Leaf Litter Critters

Written by
Leslie Bulion

Illustrated by
Robert Meganck

☧

PEACHTREE

ATLANTA

For every kid—and kid-at-heart—
who can't resist turning over a rock

—L. B.

For my mom, who loved all living things—
no matter how small

—R. M.

Published by
PEACHTREE PUBLISHERS
1700 Chattahoochee Avenue
Atlanta, Georgia 30318-2112
www.peachtree-online.com

Edited by Vicky Holifield
Design and composition by Robert Meganck
Art direction by Nicola Simmonds Carmack

The illustrations were rendered digitally.

Printed in September 2017 by R.R. Donnelley, China
10 9 8 7 6 5 4 3 2 1
First Edition

ISBN 978-1-56145-950-6

Library of Congress Cataloging-in-Publication Data

Names: Bulion, Leslie, 1958– | Meganck, Robert, illustrator.
Title: Leaf litter critters / written by Leslie Bulion ; illustrated by Robert Meganck.
Description: Atlanta, Georgia : Peachtree Publishers, [2018] | Audience: Age 8–12. | Audience: Grade 4 to 6. | Includes bibliographical references.
Identifiers: LCCN 2017015586 | ISBN 9781561459506
Subjects: LCSH: Forest ecology—Juvenile literature. | Forest litter—Juvenile literature. | Forest plants—Juvenile literature. | Forest animals—Juvenile literature. | Leaves—Juvenile literature.
Classification: LCC QH541.5.F6 B845 2018 | DDC 577.3—dc23 LC record available at *https://lccn.loc.gov/2017015586.*

Contents

Litter Critters

Between soil's grains of weathered rock,
Beneath its veiny leaves in scraps,
Amid its ribs of rotting sticks,
Soil's litter critters find the gaps.

Their world is dark; most feel their way
Through water films and chemical maps,
In stations on the brown food web,
Soil's litter critters mind the gaps.

Mixing, shredding,
Sliming, spreading,
Nutrient transfer, energy flow.

Tunneling, chewing,
Humus-pooing,
Decomposers help plants grow.

When green food webbers live, then die,
Their corpses would be nutrient traps
If not for Earth's recycling crew—
Soil's litter critters fill the gaps!

Science Note

The leaf litter layer, also called the duff, is the crossroads where air, soil, water, plants, animals, and microbes meet. It's an ecosystem hiding beneath our feet, teeming with the billions of tiny, busy recyclers of the brown food web.

The brown food web's key decomposers—microscopic bacteria and fungi—are especially good at changing dead organic matter (dead matter from organisms like animals and plants) into useful nutrients. These decomposers become tasty nutrition packets for other brown food web organisms to graze on. Still others chew and shred dead organic matter into smaller bits. Some dig tunnels, mixing organic matter into deeper soil layers. Many brown food webbers eat a mixture of foods—including each other! All of this chewing, tunneling, and pooping improves soil's ingredients and structure.

Healthy soil contains digested organic matter called humus, mixed with tiny grains of weathered rocks and minerals. The continuous work of Earth's brown food web critters recycles the nutrients plants need back into the soil. Plants absorb these nutrients from the soil around their roots (an area called the rhizosphere) and use them as building blocks to grow and make energy for the plant eaters of the *green* food web.

Bacteria Criteria

In the restless world
of the
root-o-sphere rhizosphere
we're plants' perfect partners
trading their favorite flavor of nitrogen for
the sugars
rootlet tips leak
into surrounding soil.

To get food
we exude enzymes
outside our single cells
our filaments
our colonies
decomposing already dead
plants
animals
fungi
we soak up the spoils.

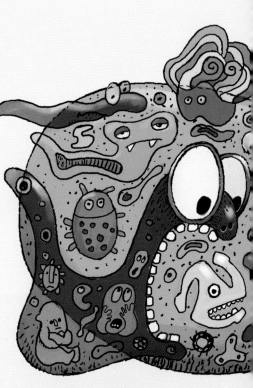

We're anchors in our
brown food web
nifty nuggets of nutritious protoplasm
that rain would wash away
if we didn't
stick ourselves to soil
with sugar slime.

We would divide
geometrically
into gazillions
overgrowing the world
if we weren't
greedily gobbled by
pesky
protist
predators
(among others)
Oh well.

Science Note

You need a powerful microscope to see the *one hundred million* to *one billion* bacteria you might find living in the water film within one teaspoon of soil. Though some bacteria make their own food and some cause infection, most others do important recycling work by breaking down dead organic matter and absorbing nutrients into their cells. Many bacteria partner with roots, converting nitrogen gas from the atmosphere into the chemical form plants can use, while taking in sugars and other substances roots leave nearby in the soil. Like a time-release fertilizer, nutrients absorbed by bacteria are safely stored in the rhizosphere until bacteria are grazed by the next critter in the brown food web.

The Mighty Mushroom Is a Fun Guy

Threadily spreadily
soil's fungal filaments
network the rhizosphere
near and away.

Rotting dead wood and leaves
enzyme-acidically,
true superheroes of
litter decay.

Science Note

Since fungi have characteristics of plants *and* animals, they have their own branch on the tree of life. Fungi send out threads called hyphae that channel through soil, scouting for sources of food. We recognize their reproductive bodies as mushrooms. Many fungi are nature's hardest-working decomposers. Their enzymes and acids can break down tough substances like the cellulose in green plants' cell walls, and wood, which is made of lignin. Fungi wastes (and their living cells) are consumed by other organisms in the brown food web. Some important fungi are good partners for plants. They get sugars from plants' roots and transport nutrients, water, and even chemical messages to other plants some distance away.

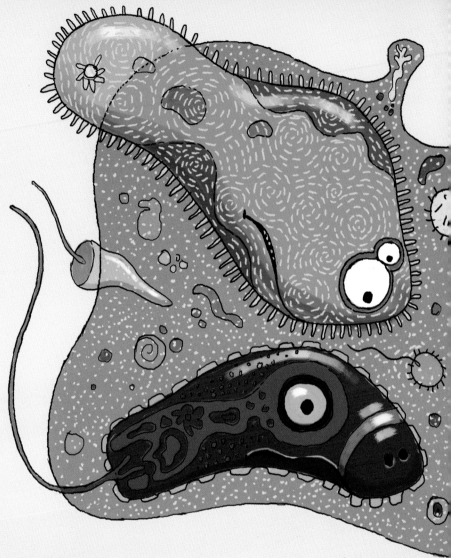

Science Note

Single-celled bacteria eaters share some characteristics with animals *and* plants. Three kinds of single-celled soil critters—flagellates, ciliates, and amoebas—eat bacteria and release nitrogen into the soil for plants to use. Tiny flagellates move through water films with whiplike flagella as they absorb or engulf food. Rows of fine hairs called cilia propel ciliates through water-filled spaces and create currents to help bacteria flow toward the ciliate's mouth. An amoeba pours its soupy cell innards into a constantly stretching, changing form to move, creating "false feet," or pseudopods. To eat, the amoeba stretches a "foot" completely around its food (bacteria, flagellates, or ciliates) and engulfs it in a bubble of digestive juices.

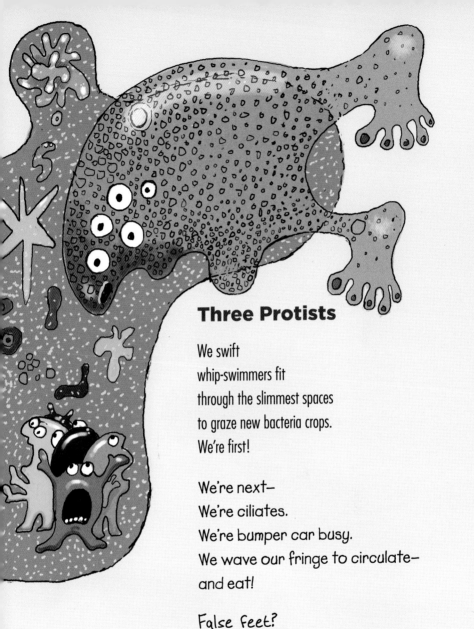

Three Protists

We swift
whip-swimmers fit
through the slimmest spaces
to graze new bacteria crops.
We're first!

We're next—
We're ciliates.
We're bumper car busy.
We wave our fringe to circulate—
and eat!

False feet?
Please! Amoebas
live to go with the flow,
engulfing food (like those first two).
Ooze on!

The Rotifer

I somersault and telescope,
Head-toe-head-toe here I go.
When soil's too dry to swim, I cope,
I somersault and telescope.
My crown will wave again, I hope,
But when I can't swim to and fro,
I somersault and telescope,
Head-toe-head-toe here I go!

Science Note

Rotifers are one of the smallest multicellular animals. They live in water, and in water films on soil and leaf litter. Their crown of hairlike cilia beats to help them swim, and creates currents to bring food into their mouths. The waving circles of cilia look like spinning wheels, which explains how this animal got the name rotifer, Latin for "wheel bearer." In less moist environments, they stretch and shrink along like inchworms. In very dry conditions, they can form into a capsule (cyst). In the brown food web, rotifers are not only scavengers that eat algae, fungi, and bits of dead organic matter, but are also predators of bacteria and protists.

Watch Out for Bears

When leafy litter's parched bone dry,
Most water critters flee or die,
But water bear stays on location
In suspended animation.

The tardigrade, profoundly plump,
Can shrink-dry to a tardi-stump,
A tun on an unplanned stay-cation,
In suspended animation.

Ten long years may come and go,
And then—a sudden water flow
Will bring on bear-tun rehydration,
From suspended animation.

Eight scrabbly legs with grabby claws,
A head equipped with stabby straws,
The hunter's back in circulation—
Tardigrade re-animation!

Science Note

A tardigrade, whose name means "slow stepper," is no bigger than a period in this poem. Also called water bear or moss piglet, it needs water to live and hunt. The tardigrade has the amazing ability to survive drought, high and low temperatures, radiation, and other extreme environments by shrinking into a "tun" (a drought-resistant form) and stopping its body functions until environmental conditions improve. By grazing on bacteria and fungi and preying on small litter animals like protists, roundworms, and rotifers, the tardigrade returns nutrients to the soil as it produces wastes in the process known as excretion. When it's eaten by its predators—larger roundworms, carnivorous fungi, mites, spiders, and some insect larvae—it becomes a tardigrade nutrition package!

nematodes

we
wiggle
through
water film
flip
flick
whip
slip
we're
quick.

with
layers
of
lips
we
sip
bacteria
and
nip
sticky
fungus
unless
it's
a   attack   (and *we're* the snack.)
tricky   fungus
trap

Science Note
Scientist E. O. Wilson estimated that four out of every five animals on Earth are nematodes, also called round-worms. Soil nematodes live in the thin films of water between soil grains, and most graze on bacteria and fungi. Their wastes release lots of the nitrogen that plants can use, directly into the rhizo-sphere. Nematodes are food for soil predators—some springtails slurp them in like spaghetti. Certain fungi attract nematodes, then trap them in a noose or on a sticky hyphal thread. It's eat *and* be eaten in the wild world of soil nematodes!

Glue Peg? Please! I'm a Springtail!

In fallen leaves
and underground,
in crannies where
soil mites are found,
these arthropods
(of jointed leg),
inelegantly
named "glue peg,"
wear bright white skin,
or cheery swirls,
and short antennae
strung like pearls.

They scurry through
the soil pore maze,
to find bacteria
to graze,
or fungi.
Mites munch these foods, too.
They're on the same
brown food web crew.

But they've a tool
that mites don't share,
a spring that flings them
in the air.

This fork-shaped tail
stays hooked below
until the springtail
lets it *GO*.
When frightened
they don't need to run;
instead they catapult—
so fun!

Imagine springtails
in a pinch
(a hundred of them
per square inch)
back-flipping, popping
toward the sky
when predators
appear nearby.

They make their
crazy leaps away
and live to graze
another day,
avoiding bites from
enemies
like mites—
their beastie frenemies.

Science Note

Springtails, along with mites, are the most numerous animals in the brown food web after nematodes, which makes them important decomposers. As springtails move between narrow soil spaces called pores, they graze on bacteria, fungi, and dead plant and animal matter. Some of the nutrients in their food are excreted into the soil, and some nutrients are passed up the food web to their predators. Springtails' scientific name, Collembola, means "glue peg" in Greek, in reference to a tubelike organ under their abdomen. Their common name "springs" from their folded, forked tail, or furcula. The furcula unhooks, launching the springtail 50 to 100 times as high as it is long when it needs to escape danger—the equivalent of you jumping from the ground to the top of the Statue of Liberty's torch! Springtails are not insects. But like insects, they are also arthropods with six jointed legs.

Two Mites

Dear Mite,
Short legs tucked tight,
you hide from ant's strong bite,
dead moss whets your appetite,
your daughters graze on fungus with delight.
But...
Long-Legged Mite has a poisoned bite
for Springtail or Roundworm tonight.
Call that a fair fight?
Not quite!

Science Note

Most mites are no bigger than a grain of sand. They can't move soil particles with their small bodies or their eight legs, so they travel in soil's narrow air-filled pores, eating fungus and dead plant material, and depositing their solid waste. Their waste, called frass, improves soil's texture and provides good surfaces for bacteria to grow. Some mites (also known as beetle mites) can pull their bodies and legs completely inside their hard exoskeleton. Many species are all females who reproduce by making daughter copies of themselves. Predatory mites are larger, and they eat springtails, nematodes, and other tiny soil animals.

Proturans **and** Diplurans

We eat debris
from forest floors,
like rotting plants
and fungus spores.

(Some of us
are carnivores.)

We're wingless,
whitish-pale, and blind
soil critters—
the six-legged kind.

We're smaller,
somewhat
hard to find.

Our advantages
are ma<u>ny</u>,
like our slender,
long antennae.

Antennae?
Whoops—
We haven't any.

Our front legs sense,
our back four run.

We've double tails.

Rats! We have none.
Our heads are cones.

Our tails are fun!
We like our tails,
since our tails lead
us to the deadish
food we need.
And some of us
are of the breed
whose tails are pincers,
grabbing prey
that's small and tasty
mites, let's say,
or...mmm...hellooo...

YIKES! RUN AWAY!

Science Note

Proturans and diplurans are wingless, eyeless, pale denizens of moist litter and soil spaces. Proturans, along with springtails, are among the smallest of the six-legged relatives of insects—not much bigger than a comma in this note. Instead of antennae, proturans use their first pair of legs for sensing information about their environment. They are believed to eat parts of fungus and other organic matter. Some diplurans are similar sized, with long antennae and slender double tails that provide sensory information. Others are larger, with long antennae and tails shaped like short, sharp pincers to grab live prey such as mites, springtails, or their cousins, the proturans.

26

Scavenger Symphylan

I'm called a "garden centipede,"
I scoot through soil at nano-speed,
My long antennae take the lead
Toward tender rootlets, sprouting seed,
Or new-ish dead of any breed,
Since I'm no fusspot when I feed.

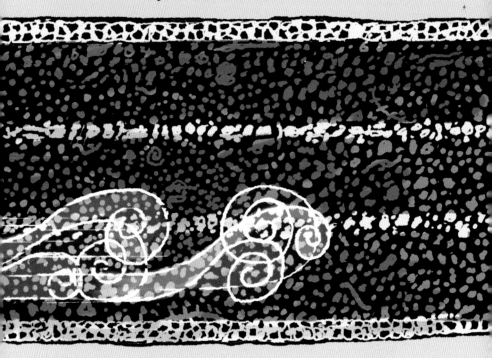

Science Note

The symphylan looks like a white mini-centipede no longer than an eyelash. Twelve pairs of legs help symphylans move quickly up and down through pore spaces and the tunnels made by other organisms in damp soil. Instead of eyes, symphylans use sensory cells on their long antennae and on their third-to-last pair of legs to scavenge for a wide variety of foods to chew, including newly decaying plant and animal matter, soil microorganisms like nematodes, and tender root hairs and sprouts. Symphylans can eat twenty times their own weight every day, so the wastes they produce help move nutrients up and down in the soil.

Night Duty

Under bark and through the duff,
They scuttle by the dozens,
They're insects' distant relatives,
They're crab and lobster cousins.

They're smallish bugs with longish names:
Terrestrial crustaceans,
With fourteen land-legs, all the same,
They're iso-pod sensations!

They're sowbugs, pillbugs, roly-polies,
Woodlice, also slaters,
With four antennae sensing clues,
They're super food locators.

This crew can chew the whole night through
In dead leaf demolition,
And then they chew each others' poo,
For extra-rich nutrition!

Science Note

Like other soil animals that chew up dead and decaying organic matter, soil isopods, also called sowbugs and pillbugs, break leaves and bark into smaller pieces. This makes it easier for the enzymes from their gut bacteria to get to work. Soil bacteria live on isopod fecal pellets, making these solid wastes extra-nutritious for hungry mites, certain springtails, pot worms, and other isopods (iso=same, pod=foot). To avoid becoming a meal for birds, centipedes, beetles, and others, some sowbugs play dead, while pillbugs roll themselves into an armor-plated ball. Terrestrial (land-living) isopods evolved from water-dwelling species and still breathe with gills, so they must remain moist. Instead of losing precious water as urine, they expel ammonia vapor into the air. Pee-ew!!

Not Much Muscle

The tiny white wigglers called pot worms,
Can be found in most any soil that's got worms.
The earthworm digs tons of tunnels—it's lots bigger.
The pot worm is daintier, so it's not as big a digger.

Science Note

Pot worms are thin, nearly see-through white worms that are typically no longer than the dash in this poem. They are grazers and shredders who chew up rotting plant matter and the bacteria and fungi helping it rot. Like earthworms, they are segmented worms, but since they are so much smaller, pot worms can't dig impressive, soil-mixing tunnels. Instead, pot worms dig slender channels through soft earthworm castings and in the spongy, duff layer of the forest floor. As they eat, they leave fine-grained waste particles behind. That is, until they're eaten by a leaf litter predator like a beetle, a larval fly, a nematode, or a mite.

Our Friend, the Earthworm

This ecosystem engineer,
Who tills the soil its whole career,
Can stick its throat outside its mouth,
And make leaf litter disappear.

It vacuums up great gobs of duff,
(The deadish, brownish, leafy stuff)
And grinds it smaller, in its gut,
Where sand stands in for teeth—that's rough!

And critters caught in each worm gulp,
Get pulverized to critter pulp.
Worm castings are the undigested
masterpieces all worms sculp.

Science Note

Earthworms vacuum up and shred mouthfuls of bacteria, fungi, roundworms, and single-celled creatures mixed with humus, soil, and leaf litter. Bacteria in the worms' gut go to work on hard-to-digest humus, releasing nutrients the worms can use. Earthworms' soil-mixing tunnels and crumbly piles of solid waste (castings) help change the structure of the soil. This earns earthworms the nickname "ecosystem engineers." The most common earthworm in the United States is an invader from Europe that can be beneficial in gardens, but they may outcompete other species and dig too many tunnels in forest duff and soil.

In Defense of Millipedes

When vexed,
millipedes
are flexible.
They will spill
awful smells,
or curl
in spirals
while
their exoskeletons
shelter pairs and pairs
of pushy feet.
They wait,
until threat ends,
until their world is wet, and
then they decamp,
seeking damp plant rot
to eat.
Sweet!

Science Note

Although their name means "thousand feet," the leggiest millipede known has 375 pairs of feet—750 total. Their strong, short legs help them tunnel through moist soil, mixing upper layers as they shred and digest old wood and leaf litter. When threatened by predators like birds and mice, millipedes can't bite or sting; instead, most curl into a protective spiral and some even ooze smelly, irritating droplets from spots on each side of their body segments.

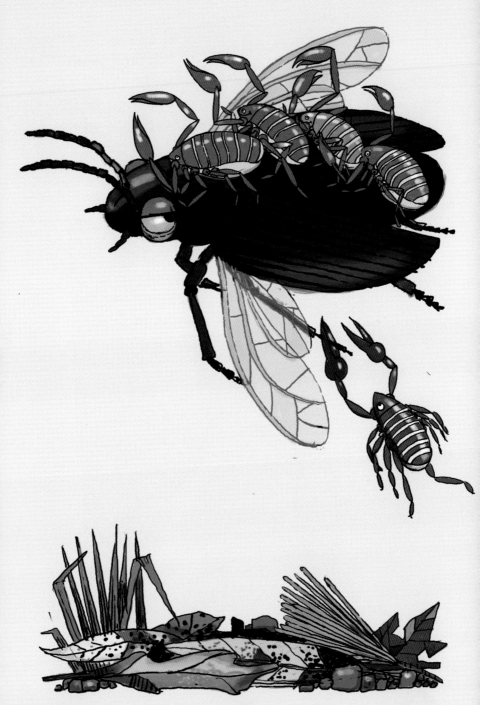

The Pseudoscorpion Life

This flat arachnid hides in tiny spaces,
Among dead leaves, in soil, or under bark,
Its hairy claws can sense a springtail's traces,
It feels its way to snag snacks in the dark.

The pseudoscorpion hasn't got a stinger,
With giant claws it nabs, then poisons prey,
But switching jobs from predator to clinger,
It catches rides to hitchhike far away.

Besides attacking prey with poisoned stab,
This critter keeps close track of passers-by,
So it can use its pincer claws to grab
A beetle's leg or wing of resting fly.

With seats on beetle buses and jet-plane flies,
The pseudoscorpion dodges exercise.

Science Note

Pseudoscorpions are tiny arachnids, most no bigger than this letter **O**. Their front-most legs, called pedipalps, are outsized claws equipped with venom that will paralyze their favorite prey, springtails, but can't harm a human. Pseudoscorpions also use their claws to save travel energy by hitching rides on longer-legged critters like harvestmen (sometimes called daddy longlegs), or on airborne flies and beetles.

37

Centipede Attack

We slither amid bark and stone,
We crawl in soil's dank litter zone,
Swift predators who prowl the dark night through.

Our many legs all end in claws,
The front pair snaps like trapping jaws,
Injecting prey with poison. Then we chew.

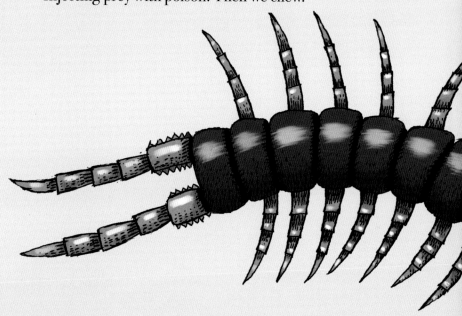

Science Note

Centipedes are solitary night predators that keep to the dark, damp spaces in leaf litter and soil. Although their name means "hundred legs," centipedes have between 15 and 191 pairs of legs, one pair on each body segment. Their first pair of legs has evolved into muscular pincers that inject poison into their prey—usually small worms, slugs, and soft-bodied insects in the decomposer food web. Once prey is stunned, centipedes munch it with their feeding mouthparts. But the outer coverings of birds, frogs, and ground beetles are tough enough to repel these stabbing pincer legs, and these predators can make centipedes *their* prey.

Rove Beetle

Velcro-tongued predator
snags maggots, mites, snails, slugs
soil pest patrol
requires a flexible
appetite *and* abdomen

Science Note

Rove beetles prowl the leaf litter layer hunting a wide variety of prey, including newly hatched fly larvae (maggots), mites, aphids, snails, and slugs. Many of these prey animals can become garden pests if predators in the brown food web, like rove beetles and ground beetles, aren't there to keep their populations in check. Rove beetles also scavenge dead organic matter. The wings of most beetles are tucked under hard covers called elytra that conceal their entire third body segment, the abdomen. The shorter hard wing covers of the rove beetle leave most of its strong, bendable abdomen free to twist and slip through tight, dark soil spaces in search of a meal. When alarmed, a rove beetle will often raise its abdomen up scorpion-style, but it has no stinger or pincers.

BEETLE BISTRO

Menu

Appetizers
escargots
mixed mites

Entrees
slug sliders
mosquito larvae lasagna
carrion casserole

Desserts
maggot marshmallows
fungus flambé

A Few Favorite Brown Food Web Kings

Nutrients locked deep in dead forest nettles,
Nutritious spider frass stuck where it settles,
Cheer for bacteria and fungus strings—
Hard-working brown food web recycle kings!

Single-celled swimmers and rotifer tumblers,
Thready-clear nematodes, water bear bumblers,
Toilers in soil where the moisture film clings,
Smallest of all the brown web's grazer kings!

Pot worms and moss mites in dark soil pore spaces,
Springtails, proturans in cranny-tight places,
Minuscule critters who never need wings,
These bigger grazers are brown food web kings!

   Fungus-grazers hunt, litter-shredders graze,
   hunters scavenge, too,
   Some decomposers are all-purpose pros,
   With more than one job...to...do!

Damp-loving isopods, millipedes crunching,
Earthworms who churn the soil, digging while munching,
Many legs, legless, they chew the same things,
These are some brown food web duff-shredder kings!

Pincer-legged centipede, pinch-tailed dipluran,
Rove beetle hunts for mite country to tour in,
Clawed pseudoscorpion poisons and clings,
These are a few brown web predator kings!

Caterpillars crawl, hatching maggots squirm,
beetle grubs hatch, too,
Some litter critters just visit, then leave,
And those include me...and...you!

Glossary

alga—a plant or plantlike organism without roots that lives in saltwater or freshwater and uses energy from the sun to make food (two or more are called algae)

antenna—one of a pair of slender, movable sensory organs on the heads of insects and some other arthropods that are used to smell, taste, and sometimes, hear (two or more are called antennae)

arthropod—one of a large group of animals with hard outer skeletons, jointed legs, and a segmented body; the animal phylum that includes crustaceans, insects, arachnids, and others

bacterium—a one-celled organism that can be free-living or a parasite (two or more are called bacteria)

brown food web—an interconnected group of organisms that recycles nutrients from dead plants and animals back into the ecosystem

casting—also called cast; the undigested, nutrient-enhanced soil and organic matter that has passed through an earthworm's digestive system

cellulose—a fibrous substance that is the major component of plant cell walls; humans can't digest cellulose

colony—a large group of animals that live together

crustacean—a group of arthropods closely related to insects but with more pairs of legs, some of which are modified for functions other than walking; most common crustaceans live in water, including shrimp and crabs

decomposer—an organism that feeds on dead and decaying plants and animals, breaking down their cells and beginning the process of recycling nutrients back into the ecosystem

duff—the layer of decaying leaves, plant parts, and animal wastes found under the newer fallen leaves and twigs of leaf litter and on top of the spongy, already decomposed dark brown humus layer

ecosystem—a community of organisms and their interactions with each other and with the nonliving parts of their environment

enzyme—a compound, usually a protein, that speeds up a chemical reaction in an organism

excretion—the process by which an organism expels waste products from its body

exoskeleton—the stiffened, external covering of certain animals with no backbones, like crustaceans and insects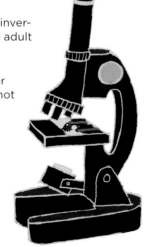

filament—a slender, threadlike structure

frass—insect poop

fungus—a single-celled or multicellular organism that is neither plant nor animal nor bacterium and feeds on live or dead organic matter; includes mushrooms, toadstools, molds, and yeast (two or more are called fungi)

green food web—an interconnected group of organisms that begins with green plants transforming energy from the sun into food

humus—the nutrient-rich, spongy, dark layer of decomposed plant and animal parts in soil

hypha—a long, threadlike tube growing out from a spore to form the body of a fungus (two or more are called hyphae)

invertebrate—an animal without a backbone

larva—the newly hatched or young form of an invertebrate, which can look quite different from the adult form (two or more are called larvae)

leaf litter—the layer of leaves, twigs, and other dead plant parts on top of soil that is partly or not yet decomposed

lignin—a rigid substance that strengthens the cell walls of plants; a main component of wood

microbe—a living organism too small to be seen without a microscope

nitrogen—an element forming compounds needed by all living cells; a component of proteins and DNA

nutrient—a fundamental substance an organism needs to function and grow

organic matter—live or previously living organisms like plants and animals; material from previously living organisms

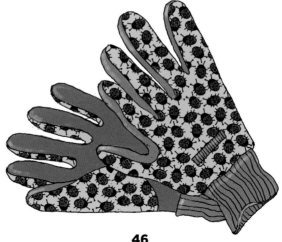

parasite—a plant or animal that depends on an unrelated plant or animal for its food and/or protection and may harm its host in the process

protist—a member of a diverse group of typically single-celled organisms that are grouped together for convenience and are neither plants nor animals nor fungi

protoplasm—a single-celled organism that is neither plant nor animal and usually can move and eat other microscopic organisms like bacteria

rhizosphere—the layer of the soil near roots and rootlets

rootlet—the smaller offshoot of a root

spore—a thick-walled reproductive cell of fungi and some other organisms that can develop into a new individual when environmental conditions are favorable

tun—the drought-resistant form of a tardigrade that can withstand extreme conditions by stopping all metabolic processes and entering a resting state

Poetry Notes

Litter Critters
This poem has five sections, or stanzas. Three of the stanzas have four lines, and each of those lines has four STRONG beats:

> Be/TWEEN soil's GRAINS of WEAthered ROCK

The third and fourth stanzas have three lines each. If you read these stanzas together, they add up to the same number of strong beats as one of the other stanzas. But adding the softer "ing" at the end of a line changes the rhythm a little bit—setting off those sections and calling the reader's attention to important concepts like "humus-pooing!"

Bacteria Criteria
This free verse poem personifies bacteria by speaking in the bacterial first person. Many lines use alliteration for flow, and many are short—even a single word—reminding the reader of the tiny size of single-celled bacteria.

The Mighty Mushroom Is a Fun Guy
A double dactyl uses the rollicking rhythm of STRONG/soft/soft (those three syllables make up one dactyl) in each line of the two-stanza poem. Most lines have two dactyls, and the fourth line in each stanza has only one STRONG/soft/soft, plus one final STRONG beat. The sixth line in a double dactyl should be one long six-syllable word.

Three Protists
This is a series of three linked cinquain stanzas. A cinquain is a five-line poem where each line has the following number of syllables, beginning with the first line: 2, 4, 6, 8, 2.

The Rotifer
A triolet is an eight-line poem with only two rhyme sounds. The first line, the fourth line, and the seventh line are exactly the same, and they also rhyme with the third and fifth lines, so the poet has to come up with a good rhyming sound for that one! The second line rhymes with the sixth and is repeated as the eighth line.

Watch Out for Bears
A kyrielle is a poem made of four-line stanzas. The fourth line is a refrain—a line that's repeated in each stanza. Each stanza in this poem has two rhyming couplets, but in a kyrielle the poet can also rhyme first lines with third lines, and second lines with fourth lines.

nematodes
The poem "nematodes" is written in free verse with no set pattern, and it uses lots of short, quick sounds to mimic the flickery movements of a nematode through the soil. It is also a shape poem, with words that wiggle and bend like a worm. The last few words curl around—just like the trap of a strangler fungus!

Glue Peg? Please! I'm a Springtail!
This poem has short, snappy lines to remind the reader of the short, cute, jumping bodies of springtails.

Two Mites
The rubliw is a nine-line poetic form invented by the American poet Richard Wilbur but named by another poet friend who spelled Wilbur backwards. Each poem starts with "Dear _____," a line with two syllables and one strong beat. The second line has two strong beats. Each line increases one beat until there are five strong beats, then lines six through nine decrease back to one strong beat. All nine lines end with the same rhyme sound.

Proturans and Diplurans
"Proturans and Diplurans" is a poem in two voices. The voice on the left is the smaller proturan talking. The voice on the right is the larger dipluran. The lines in the center column represent both of these animals speaking together.

Scavenger Symphylan
A monorhyme is a rhyme scheme with only one rhyme sound. "Scavenger Symphylan" is a one-stanza, six-line monorhyme all sprung from the word centipede, which a symphylan isn't!

Night Duty
"Night Duty" is a series of four ballad stanzas. A ballad stanza is a four-line stanza in which the first and third lines have four strong beats like the line:

UNder BARK and THROUGH the DUFF.

These lines can rhyme but don't have to. The second and fourth lines rhyme, and have three strong beats, as in the following line:

They SCUttle BY the DOzens.

In "Night Duty" the first and third lines all end on a STRONG beat and the second and fourth lines all end on a soft beat, like the word DOzens. Many songs are written in ballad stanzas. Try clapping out the strong beats of "Row, Row, Row Your Boat."

Not Much Muscle
A clerihew is a funny four-line poem that doesn't have any rules about number of beats or syllables. The first line of a clerihew has to end with the name of the poem's subject, which is usually a person, but in this case is a pot worm. The second line ends with a rhyme for that name to make a rhyming couplet. It was a challenge to rhyme something with POT worms, so I used a two-word combo where I wanted to STRESS the first word: GOT worms! The third and fourth lines in a clerihew rhyme with each other—another couplet.

Our Friend, the Earthworm
The lines in this poem each have four strong beats. Each stanza has four lines. The first, third, and fourth lines in each stanza rhyme with each other.

In Defense of Millipedes
This poem is free verse using rhyme, partial-rhyme (also called off-rhyme), and repetitive sounds to lead the reader along. The sound of the letter *L* in the word mi*l*ipede, for example, is repeated in flexib*l*e, sme*ll*, coi*l*, spira*l*, exoske*l*eton, she*l*tering and wor*l*d. Can you find another repetitive sound in the poem?

The Pseudoscorpion Life
The solemn—and some might say gruesome—life of an arachnid inspired this Shakespearean sonnet. The form is built around fourteen lines—three quatrains of four lines each that rhyme every other line, plus a final rhyming couplet. Each line has five beats in the pattern soft-STRONG, called iambic pentameter.

Centipede Attack
"Centipede Attack" has two stanzas with three lines each. The first two lines in each stanza have four strong beats, and they rhyme with each other—forming a rhyming couplet. The third line in each stanza has five strong beats, and these two final lines rhyme with each other, connecting the stanzas.

Rove Beetle
"Rove Beetle" is a tanka—a poetic form developed in Japan more than a thousand years ago. A tanka is made from five short lines and has no more than thirty-one syllables. If you read lines 1–3 of a tanka, or lines 3–5 of the same tanka, each set should present a complete image. The middle line, line 3, is considered a turning point.

A Few Favorite Brown Food Web Kings
This poem uses the rhythm and rhyme pattern of the song "My Favorite Things," composed by Richard Rodgers and Oscar Hammerstein for the musical play *The Sound of Music*. Each of the three four-line stanzas in this poem lists many of the soil and leaf litter critters from the earlier poems, grouped by their job in the leaf litter. The stanzas with three lines follow the rhythm and rhyme of the original song's refrain.

LITTER CRITTER INVESTIGATIONS

(Note: in cooler climates, this activity is best from late spring to early fall)

Materials you will need

a trowel

garden gloves or rubber gloves to wear while digging

clean, repurposed clear plastic food containers with lids

a magnifying glass

toothpicks, Popsicle sticks, a spoon

black construction paper, white paper

nonchlorinated water

vinyl exam gloves to handle specimens

a gooseneck lamp or a flashlight

a blank notebook

optional: dissecting microscope, petri dishes

Important: Use recommended local preventive measures to avoid bites from ticks, mosquitoes, and other pests. Wash hands after all field and lab work.

A. DUFF SAMPLING

In the field

Choose a sample site in a pesticide-free garden bed, compost pile, vacant lot, or wooded area where a small amount of digging will be okay. Use a trowel to scrape away most leaves, pine needles, or mulch from the soil surface. Collect about 1/2 cup of soil with soft humus in your container. Record the date and sampling location in your notebook.

In the lab

1. Without a magnifying glass: Examine your sample slowly, moving soil and duff gently with toothpicks or other tools. Larger critters you may see include earthworms, beetles, centipedes, millipedes, spiders, and larval forms of insects like flies and beetles.

2. With a magnifying glass: Spread about a tablespoon of your sample onto your container lid or into a petri dish. Look carefully, using your tools. Is anything moving? You may see mites, springtails, pot worms, isopods, or pseudoscorpions. Do you see light-colored threads of fungal hyphae?

3. Under the microscope: In a petri dish, examine about a teaspoon of your sample. Additional critters you may see include proturans, diplurans, or symphylans. If you add a small amount of water to your sample, you may also observe nematodes, rotifers, or tiny protists swimming or floating on the surface.

Take your time observing your sample. What colors and shapes do you see? Watch for movement. Record your observations in your science journal using words, numbers, and sketches. Observational drawing helps you take a long, close look at your subjects.

Note: Pale creatures are easier to see against a dark background, such as a small piece of black paper placed under your clear sample dish. Darker critters show up more easily on a light background. Adjust your microscope's focus to observe the upper and lower portions of your sample.

You'll find a link to instructions for making a leaf litter sample sifter from an empty plastic bottle in the Resources section on page 53.

B. TARDIGRADE AND ROTIFER HUNT

(Requires a microscope; 15–45x magnification works well.)

In the field

Scrape a tablespoon-sized sample of moist lichen (These critters live in soil and leaf litter but are easier to find in lichen) from a tree or rock into your clear container. Record the date and your sampling location in your notebook.

In the lab, we will coax critters out of the sample with water.

1. Add just enough water to your container or petri dish to cover your sample and prevent it from drying out.

2. Allow your sample to sit overnight, loosely covered.

3. Next day, stir the moss or lichen around with a spoon or Popsicle stick. Press it vigorously several times.

4. Slide a piece of black construction paper under your clear sample container and place it under the microscope lens, shining your flashlight or lamp to light it from the lower side of your sample.

5. Focus on the bottom of the container. Tardigrades and rotifers are mostly transparent, so finding them takes patience. Rotifers stretch then shrink as they inch along, or they stand on end with two cilia wheels extended. Tardigrades appear as clear crescents with scrabbling legs. Watch for the flicking movements of nematodes and for mites' wiggling legs.

6. Record observations in your science journal.

7. Repeat steps 2–6.

RESOURCES FOR FURTHER INVESTIGATION

American Museum of Natural History. "Life in the Leaf Litter." *https://goo.gl/SjY3Me*
(Concise and beautifully illustrated overview PDF of the brown food web. Available in Spanish and English.)

Massey University. "Soil Bugs: An Illustrated Guide to New Zealand Soil Invertebrates." *http://soilbugs. massey.ac.nz/index.php*
(Photo illustrations and descriptions of critter biology and ecology are helpful for understanding any soil ecosystem.)

Silverstein, Alvin and Virginia Silverstein. *Life in a Bucket of Soil.* Mineloa, NY: Dover Publications, Inc., 2000. (A slim volume filled with descriptions, drawings, diagrams and suggestions for readers who want further hands-on experiences with soil critters.)

University of Rhode Island School Garden Initiative. "Constructing a Berlese Funnel for Collecting Soil Invertebrates." https://goo.gl/fb4HrA (Step-by-step instructions for making a leaf litter sample sifter from a soda bottle or milk jug.)

USDA Natural Resources Conservation Service. "Soil Biology Primer." https://goo.gl/UJBCgn (Eight clearly organized chapters detail the major participants in the soil food web. Includes overview diagrams and microscope photography.)

earthworm

Each of my litter critter friends on this page represents the middle of its range of sizes.

centipede

millipede

rove beetle

Critter Comparisons: Relative Sizes

sowbug

pot worm

symphylan

pseudoscorpion

pin

springtail

predatory mite

beetle mite   dipluran   proturan

pin

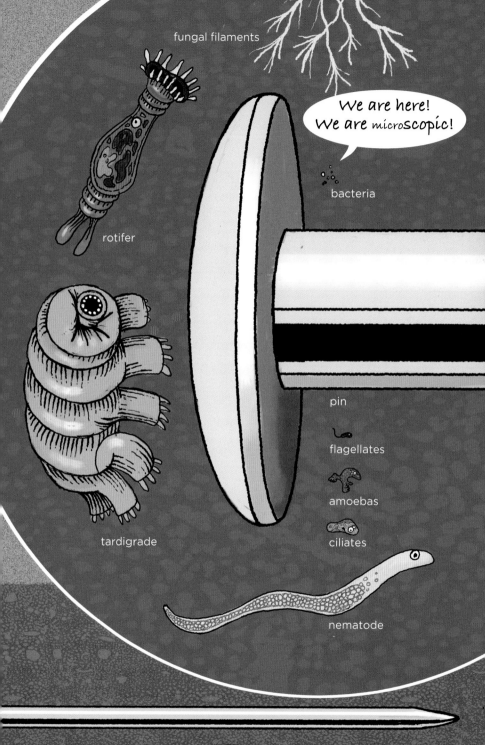

This kid-at-heart is grateful each day of my life for our beautiful, fascinating, critter-filled planet Earth.

—L. B.

Acknowledgments

I am so thankful for the continued willingness of Dr. Cole Gilbert to lend his ecological expertise *and* poetic ear to my science poetry manuscripts. Thanks also to Dr. Rick Hoebeke who, with Dr. Gilbert, introduced me to leaf litter explorations with a Berlese funnel—so fun! None of this would have happened without the learning opportunities available through Cornell's Adult University, a program I refer to with great fondness as "summer camp for grown-ups."

I met Dr. Diane Nelson when updating *At the Sea Floor Café: Odd Ocean Critter Poems,* just after the world's sad loss of her convict fish colleague, "Shark Lady," Dr. Genie Clark. What luck to find out that Dr. Nelson is a generous, world-renowned tardigrade expert who reviewed my water bear poem and forwarded beautiful scanning electron microscope (SEM) photos to boot. Thank you, Dr. Nelson!

As always, I would like to express my tremendous appreciation for the family of folks at Peachtree who attend to every book production detail (including the ridiculously challenging pages I tend to create) with such care and enthusiasm. And a HUGE huzzah for Robert Meganck, whose creative critters and problem-solving presto made this book a work of collaborative joy!

Finally, an ecosystem of thanks to Doe B., Mary-Kelly B., Lorraine J., Leslie C., Kay K., Judy T., and Nancy W.— I couldn't do any of *this* without all of *you.*

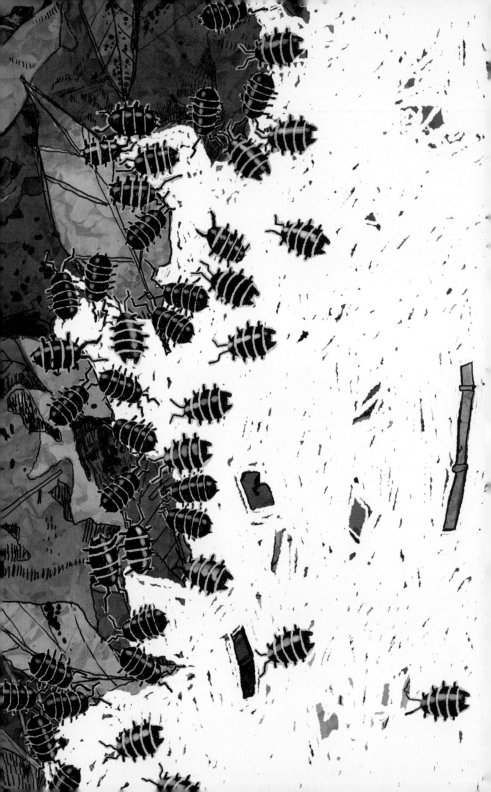